D1446786

EDMOND ROSTAND

THE LAST NIGHT
OF
DON JUAN

A Dramatic Poem
Translated by T. Lawrason Riggs
With an Introduction by William Lyon Phelps

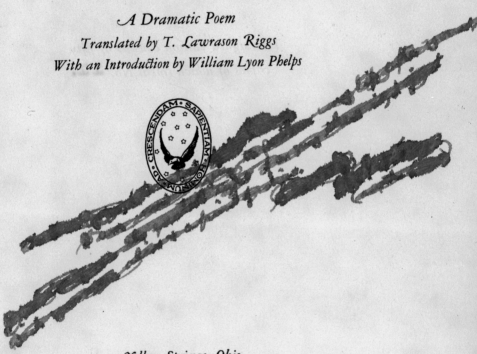

Yellow Springs, Ohio
KAHOE & COMPANY
1929

Published under the authorization
of M. Jean Rostand

Copyright 1929
By KAHOE & COMPANY
All Rights Reserved

*This signed edition consists of fifty
copies of which this is No.* 22.

Printed in the United States of America by
The Antioch Press, Yellow Springs, Ohio.

CONTENTS

SPEECH BEFORE THE CURTAIN

EDMOND ROSTAND, the greatest dramatic poet since Goethe, died in 1918; he left in manuscript a dramatic poem in two acts, which he had completed before the outbreak of the war in 1914. In *La Dernière Nuit de Don Juan* he had selected not only a subject of appalling difficulty, but had issued a challenge to the twentieth century at its strongest and most fortified position. For Don Juan, instead of remaining the showiest of villains, had become the most admired and envied of heroes. Rostand, the dramatist, the poet, the humorist, the idealist, undertook to prove that the "angels kept their ancient places," and that Schopenhauer was right when he declared that everything represented by Don Juan was an illusion. The greatest of these is not lust, but love. Lust is ignorance, love is knowledge.

Rostand succeeded not by pretending that Don Juan's way was unattractive; it was only by giving his philosophy its full value that it could successfully be attacked. After allowing Don Juan to speak for himself, to plead his own case, the final truth appears. The tragedy of self-deception is that it does not last. Eventually the chill wind of doubt penetrates the gay assurance of even the boldest, bravest, proudest, and most self-satisfied of men.

"This might be wise, to ponder well,
In seeking fire we might find hell."

In the season of 1925-1926, I saw this play presented in English at the Greenwich Village Theatre in New York. The stage effects, the acting, and the presentation were not equal to the occasion; the jewel had a poor setting. Yet even under untoward circumstances, the beauty of the play, like the beauty of a figure in ill-fitting garments, was so manifest, that George Jean Nathan, who cannot be accused of over-enthusiasm for anything, remarked, "The life of the theatre lies in plays like this. For one such, a thousand deadly evenings are gladly endurable."

I welcome this new translation by T. Lawrason Riggs, and I hope that to readers the curtain will seem to rise on a great play. Goethe said that three qualities are necessary for a masterpiece that shall hold the stage—human interest, ideality, and humour—represented by the Manager, the Poet, and the Clown; Edmond Rostand exhibited in his masterpieces these three qualities to a supreme degree; he was a theatrical craftsman, he was a poet, he was a humorist. Mr. Riggs, a scholar and a literary artist, has done his work so well that he has preserved not only the meaning, but the spirit of the original.

WILLIAM LYON PHELPS

CHARACTERS

—

DON JUAN

SGANARELLO

THE DEVIL

A BEGGAR

THE WHITE GHOST

THE THOUSAND AND
THREE GHOSTS

PROLOGUE

PROLOGUE

(A narrow spiral staircase, dimly lit, reaches from the proscenium to the stage, where it sinks into an abyss. A green and sulphurous light dapples its lower steps. At the curtain's rise, the Statue of the Commander is ponderously descending, holding the arm of Don Juan, who is magnificently calm.)

DON JUAN

Let go my wrist! Let me go down alone!

(reciting a name at each step)

Laura — Ninon — Jane — Agnes — Martha —

(A dog is heard, howling.)

Hark!

My spaniel's crying for me — charming beast!

(He continues downwards.)

Armande — Elvira — Prithee let me pause,
My lord Commander, that my varlet's voice,
Always so deferential, may descend
In faithful sorrow, to my ear!

SGANARELLO'S VOICE

My wages!

DON JUAN

May I go up again, sir, for a trice,
To pay him what I owe?

1

THE STATUE
Yes, I can wait.

DON JUAN
A thousand thanks!

(*He goes up.*)

THE STATUE
Will he come back?

DON JUAN
(*coming down*)
That's done!
I kicked him in the rump as he deserves.

THE STATUE
You have come back?

DON JUAN
That did me good; I'll burn
The better for it!

THE STATUE
You're afraid of naught,
Don Juan, and my warrior's heart responds
To courage. Come, I'll set you free. Ascend!

DON JUAN
You should have said so sooner; now I feel

2

Something that grips my cloak; a talon grasps
Its silken hem —
                    (*to the huge Claw*)
                              The Devil, I presume!
(*A cock crows in the distance.*)

THE STATUE
Dawn breaks, Don Juan, and that brazen cry
Constrains me to regain my pedestal.
Try to escape that claw.
                    (*He goes up.*)

DON JUAN
                              Indeed I shall!
Leave the tomb open, pray, as you go out.
                    (*gently pulling at his cloak*)
Well, claw, you really have no grounds for pique
Because that marble worthy let me go.
Give me but five years more, or, better, ten!
I've no small store of evil yet to do.
That moves you, eh? Come now, between ourselves,
You must admit my list is still but brief.
It's worth your while to make a deal with me,
Claw! I am he who makes them do the Act,
The best shot for your game. Besides — come now,
Let go my cloak — I'm not the same
As Doctor Faustus, who was satisfied

3

To clasp a little German working girl,
And who, dismayed at having got a child,
Called on an Angel for the final scene!
The spectre's hand has seared my arm with flames,
I'd like to show the ladies my tattooing!
Let go the cloth, my lord, and I'll go far.
Spanish infantas need me, where they lie
Slumbering beneath their white mosquito-nets.
As a corruptor, am I not your vicar?
Come now, let go!

(*The Claw relinquishes its grasp, and
disappears.*)

At last! Ten years! Enough!
Your Grace may come to fetch me in ten years,
Relying on me as I do on you.

(*as he goes up*)

Angelica — Rose — Liza —

(*off-stage*)

Sganarello!

CURTAIN

4

THE FIRST PART

THE FIRST PART

(Ten years later. A palace in Venice. A great hall opening on to the Adriatic to which descend steps of marble. A table set for a banquet, lighted with candelabra, is in the middle).

DON JUAN

Lucinda — Arabella — Isabelle —

SGANARELLO

Ten years have passed, sir.

DON JUAN

                      What a night it is!
A moment since I left the Grand Canal —

SGANARELLO

So?

DON JUAN

— On whose waters, rose and brown, each bark
Trails after it a carpet. The lagoon,
Like Madam Potiphar with Joseph's cloak,
Seizes, it seems, each carpet. But the wave
In this deserted spot, green, full of guile,
Slumbers, 'neath skies of turquoise and of sulphur,
Like virtue ere my coming. I am fond
Of sleeping waters. Canst thou tell me why
The Adriatic interests me so?

7

SGANARELLO

No.

DON JUAN

She is married.

SGANARELLO

So?

DON JUAN

The doge's wife!
He is her husband, I her paramour.
Lagoon, I understand thee!

SGANARELLO

So it seems.

DON JUAN

I wish, in order that this wave may be
My mistress, also to cast in a ring —
With my left hand.

(*Throws a ring into the water.*)

SGANARELLO

(*alarmed*)

The ruby?

DON JUAN

No, the ring
Of glass.

8

SGANARELLO

So?

DON JUAN

Yes.

SGANARELLO

What? Hers? That lady's? But —

DON JUAN

Yes.

SGANARELLO

Finished? Over?

DON JUAN

(ignoring him)

City of the frail —
Venice, 'tis that thou art! Thy stones are lace,
Thy columns stucco, every wall a mirror,
And every street a river. When a ring
Is given by a gallant, Sganarello,
The ring has wit enough to be of glass.

SGANARELLO

Ten years have passed and you —

DON JUAN

I persevere.

SGANARELLO

Tonight?

9

DON JUAN

There is a ball.

SGANARELLO

                              And then you will
Come home?

DON JUAN

                    No, stronger than great Hannibal,
I'll cull the fruits of victory.

SGANARELLO

                                        But, sir,
If the hour comes, surely such fine bravado —
                    (*A clock strikes.*)

DON JUAN

Speak of the hour, and hear it strike!

SGANARELLO

                                        Oh, sir!

DON JUAN

Hush! Listen to the campanile's voice.

SGANARELLO

Is it worth while, sir, to remain in Venice
Forever, just to have the fun of calling
Clock-towers campaniles?

10

442807

DON JUAN

But I love

The white shoes of Venetian girls, I like
To have for go-between a gondolier,
Singing, composing verses, hinting. Here
The ladies bathe in cedar, that would put
Hippolytus at Phaedra's mercy. Here
Are many opportunities, like balls,
Regattas, and processions. I love Venice!
Besides, her lion, with doves around his feet,
Renouncing scornfully the sea's domain
For that of love, resembles me. Ah, yes,
Wishing like thee, thou city mad and deep,
To live on my reflection, I have built
Upon the wave!

SGANARELLO

The city's mortal, though.

DON JUAN

Though such thou be, city where comes at last
Every adventurer who fain would break
A perfect crystal goblet as he dies,
I shall not flee to grayer skies. Seville,
A town of love, beheld my earliest days,
My last must see a town of love. Don Juan
Must have for epitaph: "*Born in Seville
And died in Venice.*" But I speak not thus

To frighten thee. The Devil, I presume,
Must have forgot us!

SGANARELLO

Us?

DON JUAN

That's true, not thee.
Thou art the heir.

SGANARELLO

(*eagerly*)
Of what?

DON JUAN

Of having been
My man. For thy deserts will have great weight
With noble lords when thou dost say "I served
Messer Don Juan!" As for ladies —

SGANARELLO

What?

DON JUAN

Thou shalt not lack, thou'lt always find a master —
And mistresses.

SGANARELLO

How

DON JUAN

                    Yes, my worthy friend,
Ladies, that dote upon my shadow, when
Don Juan's absent, with his varlet lie.
Good, angry reckoner of hearts that beat
The faster for me, what's the total score?
One thousand and — and —

SGANARELLO

           Three! And that's enough!

DON JUAN

I've never felt more keen to add another!
Today I went to all the gilders' booths
In search of caskets for my billet-doux.
Tonight I feel as though my heart were made
Of scarlet lacquer, limned with Chinamen,
Such as they make, in gold. — To supper! Ah!
All is of gold! I see my life — Why, here
They even gild the oyster-shells! Who says
The Devil still exists, thou dolt? Did not
Tertullian hold he'd died? — I see my life
In some Italian park, slipping from love
To love, like founts from shell to shell. Go fetch
My sword and mask. The future's mine. I shall —

A VOICE
(*very distant*)

Burattini!

13

DON JUAN

These old Venetian cries
Have endless charm.

THE VOICE

(*nearer*)

Burattini!

DON JUAN

The voice
Trails off through space.

SGANARELLO

(*looking through a window*)

The showman with his dolls.

DON JUAN

Bid him come up.

SGANARELLO

The old man from the Quay
Of the Schiavoni.

DON JUAN

Punchinello! He!
That's it! The very thing! I'll sup and look
At Punch, as old Trimalchio sucked a nut
And watched the frail doll dance before his eyes.

(*Enter the showman, who bows obsequiously.*)

14

SHOWMAN

Burattini   Li far ballar . . . . .

>>>> (*showing a document*)

>>>>>>>> My license!

SGANARELLO

Four wooden posts, an ancient window-shade,
A bag —

>>>> SHOWMAN

>>>> May I set up?

>>>> DON JUAN

>>>>>>>> Pray do, and tell

Whence comest thou?

>>>> SHOWMAN

>>>> (*as he sets up the theatre*)

>>>>>>>> From everywhere. I've sailed
All over. I'm well known to artist folk
And authors. Monsieur Bayle beheld my show
In Holland.

>>>> DON JUAN

>>>>>>>> I myself have travelled far,
As might a legend. Theatre where I learned
Of life and blows, always thou seem'st to me
A little Grecian temple set on stilts!
Ah, childhood!

15

(*to the showman*)
>Prithee, nearer!

(*to himself*)

>>>>>. Still I see

The showman lifting that eternal cloth
To ask a dole for Punch.

>>(*to Sganarello*)

>>>>Sirrah, begone!

Leave me alone with Punchinello now.

>(*Exit Sganarello. The Showman goes into
>the puppet-show.*)

THE PUPPET OF PUNCH

>(*appearing in the theatre*)

Row-tow! Row-tow!

DON JUAN

>>>Ah, there he is! Hurrah!

PUNCH

I'm Punch! I'm here! I'm there! I knock my nose
Against the wings!

DON JUAN

>>>>Ah, this has ever been

My darling drama! Say, why dost thou knock
Thy nose?

PUNCH

Why does one? — Talking through my nose,
To imitate a fife, striking great blows
To seem more glorious, I sing a lilt
They taught me at a fair in sunny France:

(*singing*)

I'm the famous Mignolet,
Mighty general in the fray,
Watch me make the ladies start!

DON JUAN

(*lifting his cup and singing*)

I'm the famous Burlador,
At my belt are keys galore
To unlock each lady's heart!

I too compose!

PUNCH

Bah, 'tis a waste of breath!

DON JUAN

Like female protests —

PUNCH

Tut, the carnal note
Was ever thine, Don Juan!

17

DON JUAN

                       What, thou knowest
My name?

PUNCH

Of course, my brother!

DON JUAN

(taken aback)

                              Brother? How?

PUNCH

In bawdry!

DON JUAN

         Bawdry? Words one should not use
Were ever thine, Don Punch!

PUNCH

                       Though of us two
I be the ruddier, thou the greater ass,
We two shall be alike on Judgment Day!

DON JUAN

Clown!

(Punch rings a bell.)

              Wherefore ringest thou?

18

PUNCH

It is the hour,
The solemn hour, when Punchinello meets
Don Juan.

DON JUAN

So, thou greetest in me, then,
Another marionette?

PUNCH

As for the "marry,"
'Tis sure thou art polygamous.

DON JUAN

Too vague,
That term! let's rather say I've wed
A thousand times. But come, restore to me
My childhood. Sing thy gamut through thy nose!

PUNCH

Do, re, mi, fa, sol, la —

DON JUAN

I see again
A pallid little boy in a great ruff,
Pallid from watching Punch among —

PUNCH

Whom?

19

DON JUAN

Maids,
Whose laugh absolved from every peccadillo.

PUNCH

Do, re, mi—

THE PUPPET OF A DOWAGER
(*appearing*)
Wretch, thou hast betrayed my daughter!

PUNCH

Thou art a plague!

(*He kills her.*)

DON JUAN

The lady came, as came
My lord Commander after me!

PUNCH

I love
Charlotte!

THE PUPPET OF A CLOWN
(*appearing*)
She's mine!

PUNCH

Sirrah, thou art a plague!

20

Thou art a numskull!

(Kills him.)

One must live one's life!

A DOG

(springing at Punch)

Bow-wow!

(Disappears.)

He lives his life. He ate my nose!

DON JUAN

How the maids laughed to see blows raining down
On simple clown and honest dowager!

PUNCH

Who laughed?

DON JUAN

The maids. I sat among their skirts
And marvelled at their beauty.

PUNCH

Were their calves
All bare?

DON JUAN

Tut, tut!

PUNCH

Oh, as for me, I take
Small joy in beauty. The philosopher

21

Bayle, was my friend at Rotterdam, and Bayle
Felt not quite sure that Trojan Helen's self
Was fair.

DON JUAN

The lout! The filthy lout! Not fair?
Her beauty is the only thing I'm sure of!
Helen, fair Helen! Where is she, before
I go?

(*A blonde doll appears.*)
Ah!

PUNCH

Thou art back from Sparta, eh?

DON JUAN

Nay, 'tis not she! Alas, the sombre skies
Of this our stifling age, have murdered her!
Helen is dead, the incomparable.

(*admiring the doll*)

Oh,
The pretty child! How came this dazzling star
To such a puny stage?

PUNCH

He is consoled
For losing Helen, by a block of wood
With golden locks! You see, sir, after all

22

We are alike!

> (*to the doll*)
> I love thee!

DON JUAN

             We have not
The same mode of procedure.

PUNCH

             How is that?

DON JUAN

To say "I love thee" is the worst of form.

PUNCH

How should I go about it?

DON JUAN

             Not too soon,
Nor yet too late! Come now, seduce her!

PUNCH

             How?

DON JUAN

It is an art.

PUNCH

A strut?

DON JUAN

             Too sparrowlike!

23

PUNCH

An ogle, then?

DON JUAN

Too sheeplike!

PUNCH

What must I

Resemble?

DON JUAN

An abyss!

PUNCH

Ah?

DON JUAN

Then she waits,
One feels that one shall have her. Then, one has,
While gazing elsewhere.

PUNCH

Ah, I see! Like this!

DON JUAN

My method is a terrifying silence.
Like the horizon, I can lead astray
Without a lie.

PUNCH

Ah?

DON JUAN
And the maid embarks.
Ah, savory moment, when the plank that's needed
For every sailing, trembles 'neath a step!
The vessel's never worth the gangplank!

PUNCH
Still,
That doesn't seem to work.

DON JUAN
What wilt thou do?

PUNCH
Suppose I made her read some naughty book?

DON JUAN
And owed her to Boccaccio? I should scorn
That method!

PUNCH
(*to the doll*)
Charlotte, just a word! No?
(*hitting her*)
Biff!

DON JUAN
We differ likewise in our means, my friend.
Don't beat a woman; make her suffer!

25

THE DOLL

           Ah?
How's that done?

PUNCH

     Why, you'll win my puppet yet.
(*beating her*)
She's honest, honest, honest!

DON JUAN

         She is dead!

PUNCH

Just as I said!
    (*throwing her in the air*)
    Hop la!

DON JUAN

        Is it not time
The Devil came?

PUNCH

    Why no, the watch!

DON JUAN

          Let's cut
That scene.

PUNCH

   What? Cut that splendid scene? Ah, well!
The judge, then!

26

DON JUAN

Cut!

PUNCH

The scene where I deal blows?
Ah well! The hangman!

DON JUAN

Cut!

PUNCH

Well, what is left?

DON JUAN

According to the time, and to one's taste,
A masterpiece should be adapted. Now
I'm fain to see — the rest can well be spared —
The Devil carry someone off!

PUNCH

Tonight?
(*He rings his bell.*)

DON JUAN

Why dost thou ring?

PUNCH

Because the hour has come
That brings the bogey-man!
(*trembling*)
I'm scared! He's coming!

27

DON JUAN

Whence? From behind? Why dost thou turn thy
head?

THE PUPPET OF THE DEVIL

(*appearing*)

Grrrr!

PUNCH

(*hitting the Devil*)

Biff! My stick is broken! Horrid beast!

(*The Devil disappears.*)

DON JUAN

Another stick?

THE DEVIL

(*reappearing*)

Grrrr!

PUNCH

Biff! I've never seen —

(*The Devil disappears again.*)

DON JUAN

Don't beat the Devil!

PUNCH

Make him suffer?

28

DON JUAN

Yes.

THE DEVIL

(*reappearing*)

Ah? How's that done?

DON JUAN

Thou'lt know when thou art big.

THE DEVIL

Bah!

PUNCH

Biff! Another stick! Another. Biff!

DON JUAN

Be calm!

PUNCH

I'm scared!

DON JUAN

Without fear and without
Remorse.

THE DEVIL

One has to live one's life —

DON JUAN

And die
One's death!

29

PUNCH

He's carrying me off! What use
Is bravery? I howl!

DON JUAN
(*to the Devil*)

So that's the way
You carry him, over your shoulder, eh?

THE DEVIL

It's terrifying, is it not?

DON JUAN

It's quaint.
How ill he bears himself!

THE DEVIL

Thou hadst done better?

DON JUAN

Yes.

THE DEVIL

Wouldst have made me suffer?

DON JUAN

Yes. That irks
Thy pride?

THE DEVIL
(*changing his voice*)

I am intrigued. I'll lay my carcass down
To hear, my friend, just how —

30

DON JUAN
Thine accent's changed!

THE DEVIL
— Thou wouldst have made me suffer.

DON JUAN
Well thou know'st
The pain of holding over the abyss
A dauntless soul! Thou lov'st to drag thy prey
By the hair, the while he clings to every column!
Thy horns, above the flame thy puffing fans,
Like but to toss a conquered struggler. Me
When thou hast taken, thou shalt not have *had!*

THE DEVIL
Not *had?* "Not had" is good!

DON JUAN
My worthy fellow,
Thou wouldst have had me raging, howling, mad,
Like yonder wretch! Or else pale, breathless, prone,
As I've had women! But, since I'm unbowed
Thou hast me not! I mock the gate of hell,
Whose crushing legend Dante did not pen
For me! My memories are hotter far
Than all thy grappling irons! I am I!

THE DEVIL
That is to say?

31

DON JUAN

A hero! And the scion
Of the Conquistadores. Woman is
My El Dorado. Fearless like my sires,
Though greedier than they, I've always gazed
From conquests won towards others yet to win.
They never saw, who fancied I'd repent,
Me, coming from a chamber. I'm a monster
Endowed with soul, a fallen, wild Archangel
That still has wings. If furbelows must flutter
When I pass by, it is that I am not
Like Punch, whose wings lie coffined in his hump!

THE DEVIL

Thou hast no fear?

DON JUAN

Neither of thee, nor thine!

THE DEVIL

Thou fear'st not flames?

DON JUAN

I kindle them!

THE DEVIL

Nor horns?

DON JUAN

I make them sprout! The bravest men have paled

32

Upon their deathbeds, to behold an imp;
But I have trembled with desire alone.

THE DEVIL

Thou shalt implore me not to seize thee yet.
I'll take thee vanquished.

DON JUAN

          Note it well! Why, then
I'm saved!

THE DEVIL

      (offering his hand)
  A wager?

DON JUAN

     (shaking hands)
    Done!

THE DEVIL

         Done!
(The puppet of the Devil disappears.)

DON JUAN

          What is this
That I am doing? Wherefore, when I've drunk
So little wine, and when the festive ball
Awaits me, do I let —

    (A bell rings in the puppet-show.)
         Why does he ring

33

That bell?

(*A light on the sea goes out.*)

Why does that light go out? I've said
Things to that puppet that I've never told
To anyone on earth! You've wasted words,
Don Juan! Now's the time —

(*The Showman comes out of the puppet-show.
He has thrown off his disguise. It is the Devil
himself.*)

Ah, so it's thou!
I understand my volubility!

THE DEVIL
(*holding out a plate*)
Pray sir, a dole for Punch!

DON JUAN
What shall I put
Tonight, into thy plate?

THE DEVIL
Thy soul!

DON JUAN
Farewell,
Ye ladies fair and frail!

THE DEVIL
I am the showman,
The old, old showman, sir. Within my bag

34

I bear a judge, an emporer, three beggars;
I've caught two senators, seizing the chance
Their apoplexy gave me, on the piazza.
Will you come in my bag?

DON JUAN

No, I can walk

Erect!

THE DEVIL

I am the showman, sir. To hell!

DON JUAN

Fool, to have come so soon! Hadst thou but waited,
That had been cruel indeed! Thou simpleton,
That prat'st of hell, and lettest me escape
The only hell Don Juan might have feared!

THE DEVIL

Nay, nay, I know thee, thou dost not grow old!

DON JUAN

Will you not doff your taloned gloves, and sup
With me tonight, since I am burying
My life?

THE DEVIL

Your life as bachelor! Two chairs?

DON JUAN

Always!

35

THE DEVIL

Two covers?

DON JUAN

Always! I await

The Devil, or — Queen Cleopatra, come
From far Bubastes. If it be the queen,
'Tis well, or, if the Devil — well!

(*Music is heard.*)

Far off

My orchestra is heard!

THE DEVIL

Always?

DON JUAN

Always!

Not bad, eh?

THE DEVIL

Let us go!

DON JUAN

My cloak, then!

(*showing cloak*)

Eh?

THE DEVIL

Magnificent.

36

DON JUAN
It had to be. Those things
Are so important.— Shall we go?
(*showing sleeve*)
My sleeve,
Well-tailored, eh? — Your gondola awaits?
(*calling*)
Ho, Charon! He still rows for you, I trust.

THE DEVIL
Braggart!

DON JUAN
I always was.

THE DEVIL
The gentle sex
Demanded it, no doubt.

DON JUAN
We're leaving now?

THE DEVIL
Not yet.

DON JUAN
You're vexed that I should travel light,
Perchance?

THE DEVIL
To supper!
(*They sit down at the table.*)

37

DON JUAN
                          Do you fondly hope
That I'll eat humble pie?

          THE DEVIL
                    We'll see.

          DON JUAN
                              Dry wine,
Or sweet?

          THE DEVIL
          Dry, please.

          DON JUAN
                    Do you admire these roses?
I'm skilful at arranging them.

          THE DEVIL
                    No doubt
They are important also.

          DON JUAN
                    Come, the setting —
These chairs are priceless.

          THE DEVIL
                    Most important, too?

          DON JUAN
Observe the bric-a-brac that clutters up
My shrine of Venus!

THE LAST NIGHT OF DON JUAN

THE DEVIL
> You're a decorator?

DON JUAN
Yes, for adulterous chambers. Do you like
The bill of fare?

THE DEVIL
> You are a cook?

DON JUAN
> Nay, come!
Who can deny the importance of the sauce
Poured on a tasty hare, or bacon laid
In strips upon a Lombard quail? The gallant
Must know his cook-book. Then one spreads
Choice bits of art and literature around.
Women are not such fools as people think,
They know the difference, they prefer a —

THE DEVIL
> Cook?

A tailor, decorator, band-conductor?

DON JUAN
Zounds! Sin must glisten, sin must interest!
Now, why art thou all black? It's useless, stupid.

THE DEVIL
Indeed?

39

DON JUAN

What made thee thus?

THE DEVIL

The inkstand thrown
By Luther at my head!

DON JUAN

I liked thee more
When thou wert clad in green.

THE DEVIL

Thou saw'st me so?

DON JUAN

In Eden! Eve was there!

THE DEVIL

Thou — ?

DON JUAN

I was Adam!

THE DEVIL

Thou dost remember it?

DON JUAN

In my dreams I seem
To see us both beneath the gnarlèd tree.
What's the great secret that was known to us?
No one has ever told. . . . . . I, the first man,

40

Bit at the apple then, and saw within,
Coiled, supple and white, as thou wert supple and
    green,
Thy hideous diminutive —

THE DEVIL
                The worm?

DON JUAN
I spat. Thou bad'st me bite another fruit.
I found the same worm coiled — I spat! Thou said'st
"Bite into others." I bit! A worm! I bit!
A worm! Then thou didst tell us: "Every fruit
Fair to the eye is but a hidden worm!
There's the great secret none must ever know.
Try now to live while knowing it!"

THE DEVIL
                   Well, try!

DON JUAN
Marry, but we succeeded instantly!
The foliage in which, since Adam's fall,
Woman has draped herself, has given us vice
By giving costumes. Soon we mortals learned
How to forget the omnipresent worm!

THE DEVIL
And hence Don Juan.

41

DON JUAN

      Hence the avenging hero,
Shouting as he departs: "Brandish thy sword,
Archangel, keeper of the garden-spot
Thy generous Master gave us, with its tree
Of wormy fruit! I give it up with glee,
I leave the rustle of angelic wings
For rustling silks. I mock the Paradise
Reserved for innocence; for one I've lost
I have regained a thousand.

THE DEVIL

        Don't forget
The extra three! Thine explanation sounds
Like old Ecclesiastes. I am bored.

DON JUAN

Since all is naught —

THE DEVIL

      Thou makest things of naught
Into thine all!

DON JUAN

      I've fashioned me a fruit
Of the sublimest taste!

THE DEVIL

       How about heaven?

42

DON JUAN

To serve my purposes I call it down
Into the eyes of those I win!

THE DEVIL

And truth?

DON JUAN

Why truth is woman, rising from a well
Of furbelows!

THE DEVIL

And glory?

DON JUAN

One alone
Exists, the only Victory that comes
And literally doffs her sandal!

THE DEVIL

So
I bear thee off, enchanted to have been —

DON JUAN

The only hero whom mankind admires!
Why, read their books, observe their plays, and find
Abundant proof! Mark with what lustful eyes
Virtue detests me! What do pond'rous louts
Expect from power, save a little while to be
What I am always? Mark the zeal,

43

The envious zeal, with which professors nose
Into my life? Who does not secretly
Admire the kiss I dared and he dared not,
Because of cowardice or ugliness?
I make them homesick, all of them! There is
No deed—despite thy serpent's hiss—no faith,
No knowledge, and no virtue, save it springs
From grief at being other than myself!

THE DEVIL

What canst thou keep?

DON JUAN

              What Alexander's dust
Has kept, the joy of knowing that it was
Almighty Alexander! Only, I
Am all my army, and 'tis I myself
That have possessed!

THE DEVIL

          Thou hast possessed? It is
A victor's word, but, dear immoralist,
Pray, what hast thou possessed?

DON JUAN

             Ho, Sganarello!
(*Enter Sganarello.*)
My list!

44

SGANARELLO

(*seeing the Devil*)

Oh!

DON JUAN

Yes!

(*giving ring*)

The promised ruby. Go!

SGANARELLO

(*to the Devil*)

Get thee behind me!

(*giving the list to Don Juan*)

Sir, shall I send word

To —

DON JUAN

No. There are too many.

(*Exit Sganarello.*)

THE DEVIL

Not a soul

Will mourn thee, not a son?

DON JUAN

'Twas not worth while!

The son of old Silenus was the first

To mingle water with his wine. A son

Of mine might water down my wine. No, thanks!

Curtain! The play is ended! Shall we go?

45

THE DEVIL

Not yet! That word "possess" intrigues me still.
I know the Devil can possess, of course,
But — man? Possess? Possess? Suppose we fix
The meaning of that active verb!

DON JUAN

Thou satyr!
I see lust glistening in thy yellow eye!

THE DEVIL

Into a mess of lofty-sounding words
I always put my foot —

DON JUAN

Thy goatish hoof!

THE DEVIL

"And so to bed," the saying is. Is that
Possession? No more terrible than that?

DON JUAN

"He knew her," says the Bible. That is it!
Possession's knowledge! Knowledge! Under-
    standing!
Thou seest how terrible it is!

THE DEVIL

One must
Have known in order to —

46

DON JUAN

Possess!

THE DEVIL

And thou?

Thou knewest them?

DON JUAN

I grasped their naked souls.
Who understood them better? Richelieu?
Lauzun? Bah, they were children aping me!
No piercing gaze ever made women twist
So many little, lacy handkerchiefs
To wads of rage! I can tear up the list!

THE DEVIL

Yes, let us tear it up!

DON JUAN

I know the names!

THE DEVIL

Let's tear it up!

DON JUAN

(tearing)

I know the name, the day,
The reason, and the lie! Their secrets all
Are there! And absently my fingers stray
'Mid all these souvenirs of eve and dawn.

47

The pensive victor's toying with his prey!
I'll tell thee tales, if thou art interested;
It is enough to make me recollect
A gallantry, that, as one might a flower,
I chew a name between my teeth.

THE DEVIL

Nay, put
These fragments of thy heart into thy hat!

DON JUAN

Note well, there's not one dame of easy virtue
Therein!

THE DEVIL

Continue tearing! Thou must make
Three and a thousand pieces —

DON JUAN

— For I liked
To sniff remorse.

THE DEVIL

Continue tearing!

DON JUAN

Lions
Touch not dead things. I touched no flesh but was
Still redolent of soul. See how we tear
All womankind between us!

48

THE DEVIL

I observe

That the whole alphabet has loved you
From A to Z —

DON JUAN

I hold the Z — Zuleika.

Here are some B's — four Beatrices — Now
It's over!

THE DEVIL

Now —

(*A small fiddle appears in his hand.*)

DON JUAN

Thou art a conjurer?

THE DEVIL

Within my pocket it's my whim to keep
A little fiddle. The old showman needs
To be a dancing-master — tra, la, la —
Able to rouse dead leaves themselves. Sing then,
Fiddle on which the Devil plays at night,
Made from the wood that mistresses are made of
Beneath the bow made from the wood that makes
Don Juans!

(*As he plays, the scraps of paper begin to
move mysteriously.*)

Dance, scraps of a drunken life,
Dance a gavotte!

49

DON JUAN

Thou dancest like a madman!

THE DEVIL

The Dance of the Torn List! — Rise on your names,
Palpitate on the ground!

DON JUAN

(*as the scraps whirl*)

Where are they going?

THE DEVIL

I think they want to fly away! Ah, if
You fly away, ye butterflies that form
His life, fly, white, o'er the lagoon! Depart!

(*The scraps whirl in the air, and, scattering
like snowflakes, fall on the water.*)

An interlude. . . . Now, on the rippled wave,
Each sweet, sweet fragment with its charming name
Grows larger, larger, larger; lengthens still,
Until it makes a sombre silhouette,
Becomes a gondola, and softly glides!

(*Gondolas appear on the lagoon.*)

DON JUAN

What is this strange flotilla?

THE DEVIL
(*playing*)

Barcarolle! —

Each of thy gallantries has lulled, embraced,
And slain, each was a gondola; behold,
Each cradling bark is couch and coffin too!

DON JUAN

How swiftly in the moonlight go my loves!

THE DEVIL

See them weave in and out, black, narrow, sharp —

DON JUAN

Still gondolas!

THE DEVIL

One and a thousand! — Two!

Three!

(*to the gondolas*)
— Come! Approach —

DON JUAN

Each is a roving star!

THE DEVIL

— Ye gondolas whose gondolier I am!

(*to Don Juan*)

Shall that long vessel with an emerald light
Come with its phantom to the landing?

51

DON JUAN
(*trembling*)

What?

THE DEVIL
Or shall I hail that amethystine light?

DON JUAN
These floating marvels are not empty?

THE DEVIL

No.

Each gondola, each portion of thy list,
Carries a woman's ghost, that from her name
Has blossomed. All are there! More potent far
Than Paracelsus, I've resummoned them
To life. Which shall I call to rise
From the ebon cushions of her boat, and set
Her white shoe on the quay?

DON JUAN

Why, several!

THE DEVIL
(*shouting towards the water*)
Come, disembark!

DON JUAN
(*taking a silver candelabrum from the table,
and standing at the top of the staircase*)
The phantoms mount!

52

(The ghosts of women appear, one by one, out of the shadows at the top of the staircase.)

THE DEVIL

All masked

With the white mask of Venice!

DON JUAN

Silver shoes,

Crush the strewn rose leaves on the marble!

(He puts down the candelabrum and sinks into an armchair.)

THE DEVIL

(dancing and fiddling)

Come,

Disembark!

A GHOST

Good evening, Don Juan!

THE DEVIL

Come, disembark!

(The women continue to appear, all alike, each masked, cloaked, and bearing a fan.)

DON JUAN

It is the debarcation

From Cytherea's isle!

53

THE DEVIL
                    And note, 'tis painted
By the disturbing Longhi, not Watteau!
Watteau the gentle is no longer there
When one returns!

DON JUAN
                            Lo, bluish silver ghosts
Ascend the watery stairs!

THE DEVIL
                            All are alike,
Each sums up gallantry in her frail gear:
The mask, the cloak, the fan, the rose —

DON JUAN
                                    The rose,
The cloak, the mask, the fan!

        (*The whole stage is filled with ghosts,
                constantly arriving.*)

THE GHOSTS
                            Good evening,
Don Juan!

DON JUAN
        (*gallantly*)
                    May I offer you a sweet?
An ice? A fruit? A dainty cake? And now,

54

Leaving your fans and roses, may I lift
Your masks and cloaks?

THE DEVIL
(rapping on his fiddle with his bow)
No!
*(Don Juan, surprised, rises. The Devil continues,
more gently.)*
Yet, though mantled still,
Each lady, toying with her rose's leaves,
May tell thee, from behind her fan, the words
That best reveal her soul, and if aright
Thou namest her, the mask will fall!

A GHOST
I was —
(She continues in Don Juan's ear.)

DON JUAN
In whispers, eh?

THE DEVIL
Unless perchance we strike
A woman who can tell about herself
Out loud!

DON JUAN
(taking the ghost's hand)
You —

55

THE DEVIL
                    Naught besides the soul!
No flesh!

DON JUAN
(*to the Ghost*)
          A regular remorse you had
Each time? Your virtue always came too late,
Lucile!

THE GHOST
               Ah, fatal charmer!

DON JUAN
                              See how soon
I guess!

THE GHOST
          Just by the way you say "Lucile" —

DON JUAN
Marry, that's it, Lucile —

THE GHOST
                         you make me think
I am Lucile —

DON JUAN
          What?

THE GHOST
               No!

DON JUAN
But —

ANOTHER GHOST
I?
(*She whispers.*)

DON JUAN
Ah, you —
(*He starts to take her hand.*)

THE DEVIL
(*rapping Don Juan's fingers with his bow*)
No flesh!

DON JUAN
I know your name! You — you —
What error would they have me make? — You
know —
The fireworks — Your mother and her dog,
Lost in the crowd —

THE SAME GHOST
Ah yes, I acted badly —

DON JUAN
You acted well, — Suzanne!

THE SAME GHOST
No!

57

DON JUAN
                    What? But you
Admitted the details —

THE DEVIL
                    They're typical.

DON JUAN
True, my career has known so many mothers,
So many fireworks, so many dogs!

ANOTHER GHOST
I?

DON JUAN
   You? — What? — Somewhat disillusioned? —
   Why?
One cannot love when perched upon a peak.
Your Highness always has been too serene!

THE SAME GHOST
No!

ANOTHER
   I?

(*whispers*)

DON JUAN
      You? — At Bellagio — at the villa —
Miss Ethel!

THE SAME GHOST

No!

DON JUAN

What?

THE SAME GHOST

I was never Miss,
Nor ever Ethel!

DON JUAN

What! — That yearning heart?
Ah, the lodgekeeper's daughter, eh?

THE SAME GHOST

No!

ANOTHER

I?

(*whispers*)

DON JUAN

That bursting heart like an enormous pink?
Ah, the adventure following the bullfight—
Conchita!

THE SAME GHOST

No!

ANOTHER

I?

(*whispers*)

DON JUAN

This time I shall —

THE DEVIL

Who?

DON JUAN

My aunt, forever jealous of my niece!

THE SAME GHOST

No!

DON JUAN

Unbelievable!
(*listening to another*)
                    Ah, you? — Those words
Betrayed you, so unmask your Kalmuck nose,
My Princess Olga!

THE GHOST .

No!

DON JUAN

What?

ANOTHER

I?

(*whispers*)

DON JUAN

It's Lucy!

You read Brantôme —

60

THE SAME GHOST

No!

DON JUAN

Oh!

(*He shoves her away.*)

THE DEVIL

Don't spoil my ghosts!

DON JUAN

They're lying to me!

THE DEVIL

Nay, they tell the truth!

DON JUAN

(*listening to another Ghost*)

Well?

(*to the Devil*)

She says nothing.

THE DEVIL

That is all there was!

DON JUAN

(*searching*)

Anne — Emma — Zoe — Emmeline — Louise —

THE DEVIL

Seek!

61

ANOTHER GHOST

I?

(*whispers*)

DON JUAN

You? — He's not looking — Help me out!
Take off that mask!

(*The Ghost does so, revealing another underneath.*)

Another?

(*She takes off several in succession,
but is still masked.*)

What, another?

And still another?

THE DEVIL

Still. She's one of those
Who have successive masks, but have no face.

DON JUAN

I am not drunk! The wine is in the flasks!
I fear those frankly gazing eyes. But come,
Eyes are not flesh, I have a right to them!
They will enlighten me! — Does it grow dark?
The eyes no longer are mysterious?

THE DEVIL

That bothers thee?

DON JUAN

They're hard to recognize!

THE DEVIL

Yes, hard, without the skin, without the hair,
Even without the hat!

DON JUAN

I do not find
Those looks like a bacchante's!

THE DEVIL

Nay, perchance
Bacchantes were infrequent!

DON JUAN

Ne'er before
Have those great, simple eyes confronted me.

THE DEVIL

They have tonight the gaze their grandams gave,
The gaze they showed when they were all alone!

DON JUAN

Thou liest!

THE GHOSTS

(*laughing*)
Ha, ha, ha, ha!

DON JUAN

Laugh, yea, laugh!
I knew you would betray yourselves! The throat,

63

The laughing throat will tell, and one may — Stay!
What laugh is this they have tonight?

THE DEVIL

The one
That rippled 'twixt themselves, and which no man
Has ever known!

DON JUAN

I knew it!

THE DEVIL

Ah, the soul —
Who knows it, who can know it?

DON JUAN

All in vain
He gambols like a monkey, all in vain —
I will say who is who — I'll take the light, —

A GHOST

Ah!

DON JUAN

Yonder! That fantastic, mocking laugh —
Angela Tarabotti, you are she.
From Monaco!

THE SAME GHOST

No!
(*New Ghosts are arriving.*)

64

DON JUAN
Still they come!

THE DEVIL
Debark!

DON JUAN
Zounds! Show your eyes! Your eyes, I tell you! No,
Stop laughing! Ah, Elvira is among you;
Surely I knew Elvira!

THE DEVIL
Seek!

DON JUAN
I'll take
The golden light —
(*He seizes a candelabrum.*)

THE DEVIL
Seek!

DON JUAN
Yes, if need there be,
All night I'll bear the light from head to head
Scanning those gulfs wherein you are concealed!

THE DEVIL
Sing, fiddle!

DON JUAN
Bah!

THE DEVIL

You're angry? Scrutinize!

DON JUAN

Yes, all night long — now, calmly! Past mistakes
Are not to count. Now I'll begin anew.
Those stagey eyes? It's — Olga?

THE GHOST

No!

DON JUAN

Those eyes
Full of romantic flame? It's Lucy?

THE GHOST

No!

DON JUAN

Calmly! I'll start again. Those eyes, those eyes —
It is — Calmly! — Those eyes — it is — it is —

(*He searches from ghost to ghost.*
The curtain falls slowly.)

66

THE SECOND PART

THE SECOND PART

(The same. Day is beginning to break. Don Juan is still murmuring names as he searches among the ghosts.)

THE DEVIL

Shall dawn reveal thee still in search of Woman,
Crimson Diogenes with thy golden torch?

DON JUAN

Oh!

(He throws down the candelabrum.)
And to think I slept in all those arms!

THE DEVIL

Yes!

DON JUAN

I have muttered names all night, and still
I roam from stranger unto —
(making a last try)
Thou! Lucile?

A GHOST

No!

DON JUAN

— unto stranger! Whirling like a flight
Of ill-starred birds, I hear these names! Not one
Knows where to light. And yet we loved each other!

The Ghosts

We loved each other!

Don Juan

All alone I stand
'Mid souls, as in a forest. All are there!
I've searched! I've searched! Now, since my life
 chose love,
In which none knows another, when perchance
Friendship had granted knowledge, now I die,
Knowing no single soul!

The Devil

Thou hast seen naught!
Thou hast known naught! Thou hast had naught!

A Ghost

In truth,
Fisher who wouldst not dive to find the pearl,
Thou hadst but what is quickly had —

Don Juan

Your lies!

Another Ghost

Since when have you sought truth? Nay, woman
 knows,
When man has giv'n the hint, what sort of lie
He wishes her to yield with!

70

ANOTHER
                    Thou didst ask
For erudition, so I talked of Petrarch.

ANOTHER
Since the exotic was thy passing whim,
I donned strange wiles as I know how to do.

ANOTHER
I saw you wanted a provincial prude,
So practiced "prunes and prisms" for the role.

ANOTHER
Since blighted happiness seemed to your taste,
I smiled, for you to see, upon my spouse.

ANOTHER
Man has devised his queens, his Omphales.
To be a woman is to give the male,
Just at the time when passion dulls his wits,
The eternal feminine, his own idea!

THE DEVIL
Thou hast but played at anagrams, and now
I bear thee off!

DON JUAN
                    Down, claws! My ancestors —
Were they less conquerors of India
Though Indians remained mysterious?

THE DEVIL

So, to possess is —

DON JUAN

Is to dominate!
My vigor satisfied the spirit called
By theologians — what's the term?

THE DEVIL

Perhaps

It's "principality"?

DON JUAN

Thou canst not blot
That fact — I dominated! Machiavelli
Was joined in me to Pietro Aretino —

THE DEVIL

How pleasant to have passed through Italy!
Nice little Andalusian light o' love,
How thou didst load thyself, while traveling,
With what each people adds to lust!

DON JUAN

I did

Corrupt them!

THE DEVIL

That's thy surest fame
(*to the Ghosts*)
When did you know of your desire for sin?

THE GHOSTS

The first day! — The first eve! — When I saw thee!
Before I saw thee I'd conceived the thought —
'Twas when I chose that thou didst look at me —

DON JUAN

Yet some were virgins —

THE DEVIL

Yes, so are they called
Who make their choice with lowered eyes.

DON JUAN

But I

Seduced you!

A GHOST

When we made thee choose to!

DON JUAN

How?

ANOTHER GHOST

By signs!

SEVERAL GHOSTS

By signs!

DON JUAN

Some were great ladies.

73

THE DEVIL

They

Make smaller signs!

DON JUAN

But —

THE GHOSTS

Surely thou rememberest! —
Everything—Nothing—Perfume slowly breathed—
A blossom crushed — A baby kissed — A laugh
Cunningly spaced —

THE DEVIL

A silence where I pass —

DON JUAN

But then —

THE DEVIL

Remember!

DON JUAN

No, it can't be true,
You're lying!

A GHOST

Haughtily thou didst dictate
Our own desires!

DON JUAN

Yet some were Cinderellas,
Fleeing distracted —

74

A GHOST
Always letting fall

A slipper!

ANOTHER
Thou hast climbed on cobweb-ladders,

Don Juan!

DON JUAN
What? I spent my life — ?

THE DEVIL
Believing

That thou wert first in hearts where I had come
Before thee!

DON JUAN
To seduce, then, is —

THE DEVIL
Like this:

"Watch me seduce the magnet!" says the iron.

ANOTHER GHOST
You are but he whom we have shared the most!

ANOTHER
Passed along with a laugh!

ANOTHER
Where is he now?

It's like a game of forfeits!

75

DON JUAN

              I imagined
That I was like a ravening wolf, but I
Have only been like a marauding weasel!

ALL THE GHOSTS
(singing around Don Juan)

Pop, goes the weasel!
Pop, goes the weasel!
Up and down the village street!
Pop, goes the weasel!

THE DEVIL
(tapping on a Ghost's heart with his bow)

Here and there, and everywhere!
(tapping on another Ghost's heart)
In and out, and round about!
(suddenly turning on Don Juan)
And now I bear thee off, duped, humbled, modest —

DON JUAN

Not yet!

THE DEVIL

Pride still remains?

DON JUAN
*(standing with his back to an armchair, his arms
folded)*

             Pride still is mine!

THE DEVIL

Still wouldst thou argue?

DON JUAN

Wouldst deny me this?

(*in a low voice*)

It is my hardest combat.

THE DEVIL

And thy last!

What is this pride that's left?

DON JUAN

An iron pride!

THE DEVIL

I'll file that iron!

DON JUAN

Iron knows it has
Some mighty virtue, since among all metals
The magnet chooses it!

THE DEVIL

(*mildly*)

So, there remains

The fact of having pleased?

DON JUAN

Enormously!

How can a being, thinkest thou, despair,

77

Who, from the vertigo he causes, knows
His own abysmal depth? Man's greatest gift
Has been to please.

THE DEVIL
                    Nay, who can tell? Spinoza
Was by a foolish woman's scorn created,
A broken nose made Michelangelo!

DON JUAN
To please is still the greatest, strangest sign.

THE DEVIL
Ask them why thou didst please them!

DON JUAN
(*to a Ghost*)
                                        Well!

THE GHOST
(*advancing, with a little laugh*)
                                Me? Why —

DON JUAN
(*brusquely*)
Nay, it may be I'd better not find out!

THE DEVIL
Thou tremblest?

78

DON JUAN
(*to the Ghost*)
Speak!

THE GHOST
                Thou hadst a pleasant odor.

DON JUAN
Of the abyss?

THE GHOST
                Of boudoirs, fencing-rooms,
And mild tobacco.

ANOTHER
                Me thou didst enchant
For the same reasons that made men detest thee.

ANOTHER
Because our sex is thy profession —

ANOTHER
                                Yes,
One never felt thee occupied elsewhere.

ANOTHER
I liked to brave so many rivals!

ANOTHER
                                Craft
Of terrifying sort was thine!

79

SEVERAL GHOSTS
And lies —
And ways of bowing — and of getting dressed!

ANOTHER
(*sadly*)
We have Don Juan as man has courtesans!

THE DEVIL
Well, if it is enough, when death's at hand,
Prince Charming, to have charmed contemptibly,
If thou art pleased by such renown —

DON JUAN
I hate it!

THE DEVIL
What's left thee, then?

DON JUAN
What's left me? What is left?
Oh, they will take all from me, bit by bit!

THE DEVIL
I pluck the Blue Bird's feathers ere I roast him!

DON JUAN
Courage is left! I laugh at all your taunts!
What though you thought me but a nondescript?
I know I ever brandished high my torch.
You may have taken me, but I left you! —

THE GHOSTS
In and out, and round about!

DON JUAN
Out, but not in again! He comes not back,
Who journeys ever onward; ceaselessly
He flings dull custom from him; he obeys
Naught but his instincts; and he makes his fate
Leap boldly over fools' moralities!
Dost thou not see that I have lived my life,
Transgressing every bourn, beyond all rules,
All law —?

THE DEVIL
I see that thou hast read too much
What has been written of thee!

DON JUAN
For ten years
I've held my onward course —

THE DEVIL
Which was a flight!

DON JUAN
What, I afraid?

THE DEVIL
Of stopping, yes!

DON JUAN
Afraid?

THE DEVIL

Of loving — thou, the famous light o' love
Didst flee from love!

DON JUAN

Afraid?

THE DEVIL

Of being first
At any rendezvous!

A GHOST

Of waiting!

DON JUAN

I,
Bold seeker after joy?

ANOTHER GHOST

Ever afraid
Of tenderness!

DON JUAN

Who loved and sang?

ANOTHER GHOST

Who whistled in the dark!

ANOTHER
(*in a higher voice*)

You fled from love to love as one might flee
From tree to tree before a skilful archer!

82

ANOTHER
(*shrilly*)

Of each new body found upon his path
He made a rampart 'gainst some former heart!

ANOTHER

He was afraid!

ALL
(*shouting*)

He was afraid!

ANOTHER
(*sadly*)

Of grief!

ANOTHER

Of grief, which, for the chiselling of his soul,
Man has a right to ask of womankind.

ANOTHER

Coward, who flaunted under outraged heaven
Brows all unmarked by sorrow!

ALL

Coward!

DON JUAN
(*shaking his fist at the Ghosts*)

Ay,

You taunt me in your vengeful madness, you
Who ne'er could be the first to run away!

83

THE DEVIL
(laying his hand on Don Juan's shoulder)
So that is why thou wert a superman,
Because thou wert the first to flee?

DON JUAN
(straightening up)
No, no!

THE DEVIL
What wert thou?

DON JUAN
Oh!

THE DEVIL
(shaking Don Juan with a triumphant laugh)
In what contortions now
Canst thou still writhe to find a destiny
Where naught but chaos reigned? Search as thou
wilt,
There's nothing left!

DON JUAN
(trying to stand erect)
There is —

THE DEVIL
(ironically)
A battle still?

84

DON JUAN
(*desperately standing erect*)

A battle!

THE DEVIL
(*coldly*)

Ἀγωνία, as they say
In Greek.

DON JUAN

My agony at least can grasp
New pride.

THE DEVIL
(*smiling*)

Like Punchinello with his club!

DON JUAN

There's left, that I have always been the one
Who seizes woman, furiously, from man —
The lover! I have never paled to hear
A man's name mentioned!

THE DEVIL

Is it not enough
To make thee pale, that one should mention —

DON JUAN

Whom?

HALF OF THE GHOSTS

Romeo!

85

THE OTHER HALF
Tristram!

DON JUAN
Peace! Be silent!

THE SECOND HALF
Tristram!

THE FIRST HALF
Romeo!

A GHOST
They are lovers! Thou didst cull
The yearning that those names left in our souls,
Marauder, slayer of the wounded!

DON JUAN
Lies!
My name is in your memories!

A GHOST
It marks
Our kisses, but not one of all our sighs!

DON JUAN
Oh!

THE GHOSTS
Tristram! Romeo!

86

A GHOST
>   E'en in thine arms,
> They are the gods, they are the ones blasphemed!

THE GHOSTS
> Romeo!

A GHOST
>   Go, pursue thy deathless rival!

THE GHOSTS
> Tristram!

A GHOST
>   Thou canst not slay them in a duel,
> Those two!

DON JUAN
>   Peace, peace!

A GHOST
>   Their glory makes thee wince!
> All women, that is all thou hadst — not one!

DON JUAN
> At least I have — this none shall take away —
> Made women suffer —

THE DEVIL
>   Yes, and understood
> Nothing of all their pain!

DON JUAN

What matters it?

As Attila the Hun laid landscapes waste,
I ravaged faces that I scorned to fathom.
I am the scourge of the most potent god!
That's more than Romeo, eh? More than Tristram?
Love means but this — one weeps, and one looks on;
I always was the one — so much is left —
To gaze with frigid eye while woman wept!

THE DEVIL

How pleasant to have passed through England!

DON JUAN

'Thus

I count my power.

THE DEVIL

Pass the plate!

DON JUAN

What's that?

THE DEVIL

(*handing Don Juan a goblet from the table*)

Take this frail shell. Each lovelorn spectre bears
Tonight, upon her mask, her greatest tear,
Frozen and gemlike. Gather them, and mark
How in the goblet —

88

DON JUAN
(as he passes the goblet)
Thank you!

THE DEVIL
— crystal tears

Will clink like off'rings!

DON JUAN
For Don Juan's soul!
The Devil will repay you! Thank you!

THE DEVIL
Now,

To speed the process —

DON JUAN
Thank you very much!

THE DEVIL
Tears, fall into the goblet all at once!

DON JUAN
Thank you! — The cup is full. How bright it
sparkles!
Moon, my old colleague, pour thy silver down
Upon my fortune! All these tears I drew
From women!
(to the tears)
So, you suffered, eh? In hell

These tears will keep me cool. It was for me
That all this lay on lovely cheeks!

THE DEVIL

With this
Thou playest now?

DON JUAN

Demon, with this I win!
To those of thy profession cups of tears
Are almost holy water.

THE DEVIL

Yes, I grant
The Devil burns himself by touching tears.
                    (*searching in his pockets*)
But here I've —

  (*Takes out a huge magnifying glass mounted
        in black steel.*)

DON JUAN

What?

THE DEVIL

— a magnifying glass,
My weapon.

  (*starting to sort the tears on the table*)

There we'll put the true, the flawless,
And there the false.

90

DON JUAN
(*starting*)
The false? What dost thou mean?

THE DEVIL
(*dividing the tears with his magnifying glass*)
False — false — false — false!

DON JUAN
And that one?

THE DEVIL
Thou hadst found
Its owner laughing with her serving-maid,
Hadst thou reentered unannounced.

DON JUAN
And that?

THE DEVIL
Shed for an unbecoming hat, and then
Applied to thee.

DON JUAN
These two long drops?

THE DEVIL
Pooh, pooh!

DON JUAN
So be it.
(*picking up a tear*)
Oh, what mean the clearest ones?

91

THE DEVIL

They're secret tears.

DON JUAN

(*showing the one he holds*)
Then here's a secret tear!

THE DEVIL

No, I can touch it. There was mere pretence
Of hiding it from thee. How singular
That I can handle all these tears, e'en those
Where a soul suffered!

A GHOST

All were in the programme.

DON JUAN

What?

THE GHOST

When one takes Don Juan, it's because,
My friend, one wants the luxury of knowing
How he makes women suffer!

ANOTHER GHOST

And the taste
Our tears will have upon his lips!

ANOTHER

Of course
The Devil easily can handle tears
Which are alloyed with pleasure!

ANOTHER

                    Ay, the tears
We wished a cruel wretch to draw from us,
Those are the ones —

DON JUAN

         To be devoured!

THE SAME GHOST

                    — Relished!

THE DEVIL

Ovid knew that in the Augustan Age!

ANOTHER GHOST

They're on the programme — flowers, sweets, and
    tears!

THE DEVIL

Tears one enjoys are scarcely genuine.
Well, hast thou still a straw for sceptre? Seek!
Seek!

DON JUAN

         That repeated lash has taught me where
My greatness lay: I sought! And I am he
Who pins his faith on hidden treasure, hunts
A rare blue flower on a mountain-top!

THE DEVIL

How pleasant to have passed through Germany!

93

DON JUAN

Who finds, reveals that he has never dreamed!

THE DEVIL

Thy greatness lay in never having found?

DON JUAN

Yes.

THE DEVIL

Ouch!

DON JUAN

What is it?

THE DEVIL

As I laid just now
My hand upon the table, I was burnt!

DON JUAN

Indeed!

THE DEVIL

It is a real one.

DON JUAN

What's that?

THE DEVIL

Why, that's a tear!

DON JUAN

Oh, even thou art splashed
With whiteness!

THE DEVIL
Come, inspect it!

(*They lean over the tear.*)

What a group
For Rembrandt, eh? — two profiles of the damned
Intent upon a star!

DON JUAN
And did a woman — ?

A VOICE
Yes!

DON JUAN
Bah!

(*A Ghost whiter and more silvery than the others
glides forward.*)

THE WHITE GHOST
'Twas she who like a tear did fall!

DON JUAN
How like a tear?

THE WHITE GHOST
Of pity!

DON JUAN
For the loss
Of chastity?

95

THE WHITE GHOST

Nay, for thine anguish.

DON JUAN

Ah?

THE WHITE GHOST

Thou art but anguish — yes, in spite of pride —
Anguish that yearns for arms to clasp it!

DON JUAN

Who —

Art thou, who put'st a star upon thy sin?

THE WHITE GHOST

The woman who describes herself aloud!

DON JUAN

Thy wit?

THE WHITE GHOST

Is but my heart!

DON JUAN

Thy soul?

THE WHITE GHOST

My heart!

DON JUAN

Thy senses?

THE WHITE GHOST

Are my heart!

DON JUAN

What is thy name,
O Whiteness?

THE WHITE GHOST

I am she who tells her name,
But in a whisper.
(*Whispers her name in Don Juan's ear.*)

DON JUAN

I can not recall
That name so full of grace.

THE WHITE GHOST

And I am she
Who candidly removes her mask!
(*She unmasks.*)

Behold!

DON JUAN

I do not recollect that lovely face.
Thou gav'st thyself to me?

THE WHITE GHOST

When thou didst ask.

DON JUAN

(*passing his hand across his forehead*)
When? In what country?
(*absentmindedly searching in his doublet*)
Ah, my list is torn!

97

THE DEVIL

(*smiling*)

I have here a facsimile —

(*He has drawn a strange portfolio from one of his
pockets and selected from it another list, which he
presents to Don Juan.*)

DON JUAN

(*seizing it*)

Ah, good!

(*He looks through the list.*)

No — No — Yet I have met her . . . she exists . . .
Her name?

THE DEVIL

Seek! Seek!

DON JUAN

Her name — where is her name? —
Ah, what a pity, it's the only name
I did not write!

THE DEVIL

Thou didst forget but one —

DON JUAN

(*to the White Ghost*)

And it was thine!

98

THE WHITE GHOST
What wonder?

THE DEVIL
Art thou beaten,
Seeker who dost not know when thou hast found?

DON JUAN
The name of ev'ry silly woman's there,
Writ fair and large, and — whence, then, wert thou
born,
When all these names turned into gondolas
Upon the trembling wave?

THE WHITE GHOST
The scattered list
Had one blank space!

DON JUAN
However, need I be
Downcast, because, out of a thousand times
And four, I missed ideal love but once?

THE WHITE GHOST
(*mingling with the ghosts on the left*)
But once?

DON JUAN
She's fled!

99

THE WHITE GHOST

(*on the right*)

But once?

DON JUAN

How now? Her voice
Grows distant? — Where art thou, and why —

THE WHITE GHOST

But once?

DON JUAN

— Must I pursue thy voice from shade to shade,
As one pursues the sound of wings from tree
To tree?

THE WHITE GHOST

To learn that —

DON JUAN

Where art thou?

THE WHITE GHOST

— in each
Thou couldst have found me with a little love!

DON JUAN

(*seizing her*)

Thou wert in one alone!

THE WHITE GHOST
                    In all I waited,
And saw thee always passing by. Our hearts
Beat for a listening ear alone, but thou
Didst rest on them unhearing. Each of us
Might have perhaps become the perfect mate,
Hadst thou but tried —

SEVERAL GHOSTS
                    I might have been! — And I —
And I—

THE WHITE GHOST
She was in each —

DON JUAN
                    Ah, no!

THE WHITE GHOST
                              Ah, yes!

ALL THE GHOSTS
Ah, yes, Don Juan!

DON JUAN
                    What a mighty sigh
Whelming their rancor, what a host of arms
Stretched out to me!

THE GHOSTS
                    She was in each! — In each!

Don Johnny — Don Giovanni — Don Johann —
Don Juan —

THE DEVIL

Shall a sudden tenderness
Deprive me of their souls? Up, wenches, go
Back to your hate!

(*He comes down stage.*)

Eternal Man and Woman
Would soon be reconciled were I not there!

DON JUAN

(*to the White Ghost*)

I would that I had loved thee!

THE DEVIL

Die, Don Juan,
Knowing that she exists!

THE WHITE GHOST

No, while a spark
Is left within my tear, he still may try
To find himself a heart!

THE DEVIL

Seek! If he learns
To love, I'm vanquished!

THE WHITE GHOST
(to Don Juan)
                          Even though it be
For a brief moment, love one ghostly mistress!
Take thus my head between thy hands, and say:
"I long to stroke—I stroke at last with love
The dreamed of tresses on one chosen brow!"

DON JUAN
I take —

THE DEVIL
          Too late! Thou wert too long the foe!

THE WHITE GHOST
Say: "Lo, I offer all myself to love." —
Embrace me —

DON JUAN
          I embrace thee; all myself
I offer unto love —

THE DEVIL
          The skilful fencer
Parries by instinct though he seeks for death!

DON JUAN
No! Now at last I clasp thee to a heart
Joyful and ever faithful!

103

ALL THE GHOSTS
(*unmasking*)
                              Faithful?

DON JUAN
                                          Ah,
The silken masks have fallen! Now I see
Their faces!

THE WHITE GHOST
                    Faces which have lied, as thou
Dost know.

                    DON JUAN
                    I know that all have lied, that all —
Ah!

              THE GHOSTS
    Faithful?

                    DON JUAN
                    All have lied to me, so each
Is therefore new! No, I have no more heart
For one, while a new face intrigues me!

              THE GHOSTS
                                          Ah!

              DON JUAN
              (*to the White Ghost*)
Be gone!

(*to the others*)
Yet triumph not, I still remain
Invincible!

THE DEVIL
The object of thy search
Was, therefore, not to find?

DON JUAN
It's possible!
For, had I found, I would have died of boredom.
Don Juan has sought nothing but the search
And his own self! Woman was after all
A pretext, nothing more! No, triumph not!
I took you but to leap above myself
To something higher, as one takes a weapon,
A thyrsis, or a goblet, or a torch!

A GHOST
Is this the final pride thou snatchest at?

DON JUAN
Yes, you have only been my stimulants!

ANOTHER
If that be so, Don Juan, what has become
Of all the exaltation we produced?

DON JUAN
Why —

ANOTHER

    If thou hadst from us what thou dost say,
Why, then, Don Juan —

ANOTHER

        Then, Don Juan, come,
What is the reckoning? What hast thou made
Of that fair evening, when, drunk with pride,
Thou camest from my gondola?

ANOTHER

        The nights
Wherein I gave thee lucid madness, apt
For planning mighty exploits, where are they?
What hast thou made of them?

ALL THE GHOSTS

        Thy reckoning!

A GHOST

If it be really true that, thanks to me,
Thou wert empow'red to leap above thyself,
Towards what goal was it? What immortal thing
Sprang from that moment?

A GHOST

        Of what masterpiece
Do my eyes make another Mona Lisa?

DON JUAN

Be still, be still!

THE DEVIL
At last a heartfelt cry!

ANOTHER GHOST
What ode has blossomed from the rosebud plucked
That morn, when thou didst leave me, from my
    hedge?

DON JUAN
Ah, you have probed the inmost, secret wound!

ANOTHER
When, ready to succumb to thee, I cried:
"Where'er thou wilt!" What captured battle-flags
Have I been brought for sheets?

DON JUAN
                    Ah, hold thy peace!

ANOTHER
Our rare Sicilian hour — what hast thou made
Of it — what fair, what arduous deed?

THE DEVIL
Stab one by one with long darts of regret
That vaunting heart that went astray in love!

A GHOST
Women have loved thee; of the perfect garden
That blooms within the heart when one is loved,

What hast thou made, O Boabdil that wastest
Thine own Alhambras?

ANOTHER
                    Men, who saw thee leave
Our arms, have hated thee. What hast thou made
Of all their hate?

ANOTHER
                    I was a queen. My kiss
Ought to have made thee king; what hast thou done
With it?

ANOTHER
          What hast thou done—I was an actress—
With sighs breathed from Electra's veil?

ALL THE GHOSTS
                                    Don Juan,
Don Juan!

DON JUAN
          Ah, what is this ghostly tumult?

ALL
If we were really all these things —

THE DEVIL
                                    Ay, stab
This futile Caesar!

ALL

what, then, hast thou made
Of thyrses, torches, goblets, weapons?

THE WHITE GHOST

Tell —

DON JUAN

Thou too?

THE WHITE GHOST

— What hast thou fashioned with my tear?

DON JUAN

Yes, rightly didst thou shed that piteous tear
Upon my anguish! Hearts are not aware
Of all their own regrets! So many chances
For greatness, valor, sorrow, came to me,
And I but made a list —

THE DEVIL

Kneel on thy list!

THE GHOSTS

Kneel, kneel, still kneel! By seeking naught but us,
Thou mad'st of us but Woman leading on
To Woman!

DON JUAN

I am cold!

109

THE GHOSTS

Of outraged love

Thou madest moments leading on to moments!

DON JUAN

Still I do not repent. — What pangs are these? —
Who names Don Juan speaks of victory! —
Yet each man has his day, when he believes
That he has realized himself, and cries:
"I am!" — I have not had my day!

THE DEVIL

Agreed!

Thou hast but had their nights!

DON JUAN

Don Juan is —

Not in the least do I repent! — Don Juan
Is John of Austria, victor of Lepanto! —
When death's at hand, wherefore does memory crave
One deed to bind us to the future? — Nay,
I'll not repent! — What are these searing flames? —
Art thou Life's lover, Death, that thou dost plot
Her vengeance? Must the fallen runner die,
Burned by the torch he failed to pass along?

THE DEVIL

Well, is the worm concealed in every fruit?

DON JUAN

Ah, if the will can carve eternal fruit
In marble — if one can, by fashioning
A thing of beauty, conquer both the worms,
The apple's and the grave's! —

THE DEVIL

                          Is it enough,
In the last struggle, to have lived, like Venice,
Upon one's own reflections?

DON JUAN

                        No, at death,
One must have known creation! Canst thou see
What I am suffering?

THE DEVIL

                  Ha, ha!

DON JUAN

                              That naught
Should have come from my breath — ah, knowest
    thou
That torment?

THE DEVIL

                  It is mine! Hell is but that!
None who create are there.

III

DON JUAN
                    Thou pitiest me?

THE DEVIL
I understand thee, but I cannot pity.
          (*starting to drag Don Juan off*)
Come, come along now! Thou art one of those
Of whom no trace is left — no word remains,
No gesture!

DON JUAN
               Yes, one famous gesture's left,
One famous word, whereby I heralded
Upheavals to the world! Remember, pray,
One day when, muffled in my cloak, I fled
The constables, and met a beggar, roaming
Across the land —

THE DEVIL
               Ay, let us talk of that.

DON JUAN
He asked a penny for the love of God —
His God — and, flinging him a piece of gold,
I spake the word which made the metal flame;
"Nay, for the love of man! — Humanity!"

THE DEVIL
Humanity!

DON JUAN
I was the first to write
That epoch-making word in history!

THE DEVIL
How pleasant to have passed through France!

DON JUAN
                                        Let go!

This time I've found my fate. Posterity
Will owe me something, after all. I met
A poor man in a wood, and I destroyed
His resignation! So make way for me!
By libertines is Liberty made bold!
I have not lived in vain. I can rejoin
That Beggar!

THE DEVIL
              Wouldst thou like to talk to him?
(*The Beggar appears.*)

DON JUAN
My gold piece glistens in his outstretched hand!
Spectre, what wouldst thou?

THE BEGGAR
                            This! To pay thee back!
(*He throws the coin in Don Juan's face.*)

113

DON JUAN
(*struck in the forehead and staggering*)
Ah!

THE BEGGAR
Yes, that present meant perdition for thee!

DON JUAN
(*as the Beggar moves silently towards him with
open hands*)
Let me explain! Now, liberty —

THE BEGGAR
(*raising one huge hand*)
Enough!
The thing's too great to need your sudden zeal.

DON JUAN
The People —

THE BEGGAR
No, Don Juan, stick to skirts!

DON JUAN
The future —

THE DEVIL
(*to the Beggar*)
Stifle in the liar's throat
His social rhetoric! Shall debauchees
Become apostles?

DON JUAN
Yet, I did rebel!

THE BEGGAR
But not for others!

DON JUAN
Surely thou wilt not —

THE BEGGAR
I'll strangle thee, for having dared to soil
Words that should feed our hope!

DON JUAN
A new Commander
Rolls up his sleeves?

THE BEGGAR
The first had hands too clean
To slay the hero of nonentities!

DON JUAN
Listen, Plebeian! I can serve thee, I—

THE WHITE GHOST
While still a spark is lift within my tear,
Don Juan can try to find himself a soul!

THE DEVIL
Hurry, it soon will be extinguished!

115

DON JUAN

Yes,

I've courage —

THE BEGGAR
(*sneering*)
Ah?

DON JUAN
Guile?

THE BEGGAR
Ah?

DON JUAN
A leader's eye!

THE BEGGAR
Ah?

DON JUAN
— And destructive genius!

THE BEGGAR
Ah?

DON JUAN

Then,

If bloodshed be required —

THE BEGGAR
(*suddenly solemn and terrible*)
That may be!

DON JUAN

I can commit —

ALL THE GHOSTS
(*throwing off their cloaks*)
A crime?

DON JUAN
The satin cloaks

Have fallen! — I was saying —

THE DEVIL
Seek!

DON JUAN
How can I?

THE BEGGAR

Thou spakest of committing —

THE GHOSTS
Crimes?

DON JUAN
Nay, sins!

I cannot think of causes to be served
While shoulders are like marble and while throats
Are roselike! Slay me!

THE DEVIL
Not a living thing

117

Grows where the goat has browsed. That's all thou
    art —
The rest was trimmings! On thy pallid brow
I print the cloven hoof.

DON JUAN
                 Ah, let me mourn
The suffering of the male! — And I betrayed
All else for that! — Some could seek other things,
And other things there are on earth to seek!
To think that flesh, a little veiled, can take
The place of mysteries! My heart was fit
To feed a mighty vulture, and became
A meal for Lesbia's sparrow! Slay me now,
Lest, pricked again by dread and sterile whims
I beg a thrill from shadows, and return
Doglike, unto my —

THE DEVIL
             Have I stripped from thee
The inmost wrappings? There's that mighty mind!

DON JUAN
Ah!

THE DEVIL
That undaunted prowess!

DON JUAN
                    Ah!

THE DEVIL
That will!
That freedom! Knowest thou the scornful word
Flung in thy teeth by Punch?

DON JUAN
Nay, hold thy peace!

PUNCH'S VOICE
(*in the rear*)

Bawdry!

DON JUAN
Scarce was it worth the dream of being
The acme of all human insolence,
If the last word remains to Punch!

THE WHITE GHOST
There was
A little more. His hardened pride conceals
One last excuse —

DON JUAN
I make none!

THE WHITE GHOST
With himself
He was at war! Who cannot love themselves,
Need to be loved.

119

DON JUAN

No whimpering! I die
At least without imploring thee — my hands
Are clenched. To hell! I long to go to hell!

THE DEVIL

(*to the Beggar*)
Fetch me that empty costume over here,
To be a dress for everybody's dream!

DON JUAN

What?

THE DEVIL

Thou shalt see the funny little hell
Prepared for thee!

DON JUAN

The monsters' hell, with Nero,
With Heliogabalus?

THE DEVIL

No, not at all —
A little canvas hell that's hauled around.

DON JUAN

The puppet-show! — I tell thee, with the damned
I long to dwell!

THE DEVIL

A puppet shalt thou be,

120

Eternally enacting gallantries
Before a bluish backdrop.

DON JUAN
                    Mercy! Spare me!

Eternal flame!

THE DEVIL
            Eternal theatre!

DON JUAN

I will not!

THE DEVIL
(to the Beggar)
Come, let's have him strangled now!

DON JUAN
(struggling in the Beggar's hands)
Go in the puppet-show? — I will not go!

THE DEVIL
(to Don Juan)
Surrender now thy person to the fingers
Of the old showman!

DON JUAN
            In the puppet-show?

THE DEVIL
Time to begin! The bell rings! Take your seats,
Ye ladies fair, upon the floor!

121

THE BEGGAR
>   Come on!

DON JUAN
I will not go, I—

THE DEVIL
>   Drag him over here!

DON JUAN
Not that foul box!— Give me the circle of flame
My pride deserves!

THE BEGGAR
>   Come on!

DON JUAN
>   I long to suffer!
I've never suffered! I've a right to hell!
I've earned my hell!

THE DEVIL
>   Hell is where I decree;
I fix its place. Some celebrated men
Are damned within their statues; thou art damned
Within thy puppet!

DON JUAN
>   Then at least
I'll mock my hell! The marble statue's dead,
The puppet lives. Within it, I shall still—

THE DEVIL

Shine by thy wit?

DON JUAN

Yes, I shall make them laugh.

THE DEVIL

Whom?

DON JUAN

Why, the maids, before their mothers' eyes!

THE WHITE GHOST

Thou who wert fit to play a noble part!

DON JUAN

I'll sing, and beat the dollies with a stick!

THE WHITE GHOST

Thou who wert fit to wield a mighty sword!

DON JUAN

I'll sing: "I am the famous" —

THE WHITE GHOST

Ah, my tear

Goes out!

DON JUAN

"I am the famous Burlador!"

THE BEGGAR

(*shoving him into the puppet-show*)

Enough!

THE DEVIL

Go be a puppet, foolish man
Who thought to mould thyself into my image!

DON JUAN

(*appearing as a puppet in the show*)

"The famous Burlador!"

THE WHITE GHOST

(*with infinite despair*)

Ah, what a shame!

CURTAIN